Nanny's Pearls
LESSONS THAT SHAPED AN ORPHAN'S LIFE

Kamiab Delfanian, M.D., M.P.H.

Respectfully;

Kamiab Delfanian, M.D., M.P.H.

Spring of 2022

Copyright © 2016 by Kamiab Delfanian, M.D., M.P.H.

This book or parts thereof may not be reproduced in any form, stored in a retrieval system, or transmitted in any form by any means–electronic, mechanical, photocopy, recording, or otherwise–without prior written permission of the publisher, except as provided by United States of America copyright law.

Printed in the United States of America

First Printing, 2016

ISBN 978-0-9976988-0-0

Library of Congress Control Number: 2016910024

Published by:
Delfan Press
P. O. Box 3018
Burnsville, MN 55337
U.S.A.

To contact the author:
Phone: (952) 892-3308
e-mail: drdelfanian@gmail.com

Davies Printing Co., Rochester, MN, USA
Cover design by Ads & Art, Rochester, MN, USA

DEDICATION

This book is dedicated to the memory and in honor of my beloved grandmother, "Nanny" Sakineh whose love and words of wisdom have always been the guiding lights of my life.

Kamiab Delfanian

Picture of Nanny, my sister Nasreen and I in the Kurdish village of Karim-Abad, northern Iran.

FOREWORD

Privilege:

This is a word that can mean many things to many people. For some it defines what few people have and others do not; or it may imply a special gift or access not available to everyone. In some way, we are all privileged. However when viewed in the context of Dr. Kamiab Delfanian's life this word takes on a special meaning.

You see, Dr. Delfanian is not like the rest of us, and did not start out his life among us. By some strange fate, he managed to survive a childhood unlike anyone's that I have ever known, and overcome impossible odds just to stay alive. Even beyond that, he managed to become an educated man, move to the United States, complete prestigious medical training at some of our finest universities, and establish himself as a leader in his field. To him, each and every day is a privilege, an opportunity to live and teach and learn.

You may ask, how was all of this possible?

To answer this very question, Dr. Delfanian has opened up his heart and soul to share his life story told through the teachings of his beloved grandmother. From his early years as an orphan growing up in northern Iran, he absorbed life's harsh lessons both physically and emotionally. Rather than become scarred and hardened, "Nanny" raised Dr. Delfanian to be strong and capable, shaping him with pearls of wisdom, humor and truth, and he took these lessons with him on his journey to become an outstanding yet humble physician and a humanitarian.

I first met Dr. Delfanian at the annual conference hosted by Vascular Birthmark Foundation in 2006 as part of a volunteer group of physicians to help children and adults with complicated vascular birthmarks. We have continued to go back every year to treat a new group of patients, each time giving people hope and treatment options that they might have never had available. In a small way, this mirrors Dr. Delfanian's life experience as a child with limited options, but when given a chance, discovered a world full of opportunities that he has not taken for granted.

I always look forward to breaking bread with my good friend Kamiab Delfanian every year. Not only am I blessed to have his friendship, but he continues to teach me life lessons that help me be a better father, husband, brother, and son to my own family.

After reading this book, I hope everyone can take a moment to appreciate what a privileged life we all lead.

Gregory Levitin, MD, FACS
Director, New York Vascular Birthmark Center

ACKNOWLEDGEMENTS

I would like to express my heartfelt and sincere gratitude to:

My paternal uncle, *Mohammad Ali* who filled the place of my father with genuine love and unparalleled devotion. *Fereidoon Delfanian, PhD* for his continuous guidance and photo archives that have given meaning to the content of this book.

Wonderful people of my home village of *Karim Abad*, as well as the breathtaking and picturesque cities of *Kelardasht* at the foot of snow-capped mountain of *Alam-Kuh* and beautiful port cities of *Noshahr* and *Chaloos* along the Caspian Sea who in so many ways were instrumental in helping an orphan boy achieve his long held childhood dream of becoming a doctor in America. There are so many of you to be named individually. You supported me with tears in your eyes, and kindness and pain in your hearts and souls as vast as the magnificent Caspian Sea. This book belongs to you.

Professional support of my colleagues at *Mayo Clinic*, *Johns Hopkins*, *University of Minnesota*, *University of South Dakota*, *South Dakota State University* and *Fairview Health Systems* as well as other medical and teaching institutions. My patients and their families that I have had the honor of caring for from around the globe.

My many dear friends whose love and trust I will treasure for as long as I live.

My loving wife Christina and beautiful daughters Shaydah (who prepared the manuscript so patiently and gracefully) and Shahrzad who unconditionally supported me throughout the course of writing this book.

Kamiab Delfanian

INTRODUCTION

I grew up in *Karim-Abad*, a remote Kurdish village off of the southern coast of the beautiful Caspian Sea in northern Iran.

One hot summer day my father gathered his friends to go swimming, but he never returned. He drowned in the Caspian Sea at the age of twenty-four when I was an infant. Due to custody dispute and cultural issues my mother left our home a few months later, leaving the care of my three-year-old sister, Nasreen and I to my ailing and old paternal grandmother, Nanny; Kurdish for grandmother. My childhood years were spent in a single-room house with memorable shingle roof typical of the era when poverty precluded more durable rooftops. The resounding sound of rain drops leaking through our broken roof and hitting the pots on the floor of our house is an inerasable memory that comes alive whenever it rains some half a century on. Nanny passed away when I turned sixteen years old. After obtaining my high school diploma, due to political turmoil I travelled to the United States to attend college shortly before the Iranian revolution. Despite many challenges throughout the years I studied medicine and graduated at the top of my medical school class. I have had formal and informal medical and surgical training in the United States and abroad including subspecialty training in vascular diseases at the Mayo Clinic and a fellowship in vascular anomalies at Arkansas Children's Hospital.

Due to my long commitment and interest in Public Heath, I attended Johns Hopkins school of Public Health and graduated with a Master of Public Health degree in international health, focusing on childhood behavioral

Introduction

disorders, nutrition and poverty-related diseases and other challenges of the developing countries.

I subsequently founded a center dedicated to children and adults with vascular birthmarks and congenital deformities in the state of Minnesota where I currently practice.

What follows in this book is a collection of memorable words and expressions that Nanny used to say as she was raising two orphan grandchildren. I remember her stern facial expressions of discipline when Nasreen and I would test her patience with our childish mischiefs.

As a peasant Nanny was not schooled and as such could not read nor write in Persian, the official language of Iran. However, I remember her words of wisdom and innate intelligence intertwined with an irony of wit, wild innocence and human decency like a whispering wind gliding across the beautiful rice paddies and lush green forest at the foothills of the majestic Alborz Mountains.

When women and men of the village would come to our house to seek Nanny's advice on social and family matters I always felt very fortunate to have her raise me despite the tragic loss of my parents.

Many of the aphorisms and affirmations in this book consist of my personal and professional experiences dating back to my life on the Caspian plateau as a child and subsequently abroad as a public health educator and a physician. Nanny's spirit of genuine concern for others and her words of wisdom will remain like shiny stars in the high sky of my memories forever. I hope you enjoy reading them.

Kamiab Delfanian, M.D., M.P.H.

My father Mirza Firooz-Ali Delfanian: A courageous man and a brilliant scholar of literature who loved calligraphy and music.

Nanny's Pearls

1. Learn to be humble; for the tree with abundant fruit has its branches down.

∽

2. Humanity does not seek reciprocity; give without conditions.

∽

3. Worship and prayer become much more meaningful when accompanied by genuine acts of kindness.

4. Success does not always go to the fastest.

5. Don't be dazzled and distracted by the bright lights; keep charting your destiny.

6. A colorful love is just that, colorful. True love has no color.

7. No outer beauty compensates for the lack of inner beauty.

8. Never ridicule anyone's dreams.

✃

9. Do your best, forget the rest.

✃

10. Be aware of those who whisper lest they may be hiding something.

✃

11. The best measure of doing well is doing good.

12. A true hero does not seek an audience.

⁂

13. The beauty of the valley is appreciated when one reaches the mountain top.

⁂

14. The most valuable things in life are often the least appreciated.

15. Among the saddest things in life is seeking what we don't need.

☙

16. An ounce of humility is larger than a ton of arrogance.

☙

17. A mentor is one who not only informs us but also forms us.

18. A word in the mouth is much like an arrow in the quiver; you cannot control it once it is released.

❧

19. Build a house wherever you go; in people's hearts.

❧

20. There is no accent nor a need for an interpreter when we speak the language of the heart.

21. Most material loss may be recovered but not a second of your life.

22. Poverty is a pandemic precursor to crime and violence and a serious threat to global health and security more than all terrorist organizations combined.

23. Respect is to peace what cement is to concrete.

Kamiab Delfanian

24. The most certain thing about excuses is that they are easily found.

25. Never make a decision in haste even at the risk of losing an opportunity.

26. Not everyone who brings a smile to your face is a friend and tears to your eyes an enemy.

27. Do not mistake reputation for character as there are many poor characters with great reputations.

⁂

28. It is the fire that makes iron steel.

⁂

29. Great people never stay in the way; they lead the way.

30. The greatest character of a person is manifested in how he handles defeat.

31. Expect to sink when you step in the marshland.

32. Sometimes you've got to call your mother's lover, "uncle".

33. What pleases the eyes does not always please the heart.

Nanny's Pearls

34. Independence does not mean isolation; everyone needs the help of others.

⁂

35. The value of a compromise in any negotiation rests in understanding a different point of view.

⁂

36. The best judge of your character is the person in the mirror.

37. Material wealth may bring comfort but personal fulfillment comes with giving.

38. Measuring someone's value on the basis of material possession is much like looking at a flower garden through a key hole.

39. Knowledge and wisdom are not synonymous. The world is full of skilled fools.

40. As a matter of principle respect everyone but bow to nobody.

⁂

41. Recognize your limitations: not every problem has a solution.

⁂

42. Be diligent in work and strive for excellence.

43. "Constructive criticism" is a misnomer. Try to genuinely help people by guiding and supporting them as they overcome their challenges.

⁂

44. To maintain peace there are many a things better left unsaid.

⁂

45. Praise for a child is like water to a blossoming flower.

46. Your character is your best asset; don't play with it.

47. Time is a great equalizer; it spares no one. Spend it wisely.

48. Opportunity may favor a prepared mind but sheer determination favors every mind.

49. Mingling with the crows and soaring with the eagles is a matter of attitude.

50. Once you determine that your goal has a value, stop looking for any further confirmation of purpose.

51. The eyes tear when the heart breaks.

Nanny's Pearls

52. It is not always the position and power that matters; for a loud wave may ride high but a silent pearl sits humble at the bottom of the ocean.

⁂

53. Never measure your success by someone else's tape.

⁂

54. Forgetting the past is foolish; living in the past is worse.

Kamiab Delfanian

My paternal uncle Mohammed-Ali Delfanian: A strong pillar of support for my sister and I during our most challenging days as orphans.

Nanny's Pearls

55. Allow yourself to shed a tear or two, sometimes.

&

56. False friends and snow have something in common: the higher the temperature the faster the evaporation rate.

&

57. There are times when your silence speaks louder than your words.

58. A caring mentor enlightens us like the rays of the sun without expectation.

∽

59. With high emotions, slow the motion.

∽

60. When entering a room full of people, acknowledge everyone by making eye contact.

61. Remember that the people who benefit the world most remain anonymous.

⁂

62. You can spot a politician when there is diarrhea in words and constipation in action.

⁂

63. This life is not a rehearsal; live it with all your heart.

64. The most important thing to remember in life is: not forget to live.

∽

65. A loyal friend is like the warmth of a mountain-top cabin in the cold of winter.

∽

66. Be careful with how you approach others; you can't always fix what you break.

Nanny's Pearls

67. There is a fine line between a clever and a crook.

⌘

68. Don't fancy yourself in becoming a member of the elite; we all bleed when cut.

⌘

69. "Don't put all your eggs in one basket" is a major understatement.

70. Leadership is the desire and the ability to bring people together for a common cause.

⁂

71. To be human is to strive to alleviate the suffering of others.

⁂

72. To give out of pity is human; to give out of conviction is divine.

Nanny's Pearls

73. A leader will be ineffective if he or she lacks the love, vision or wisdom to serve.

∽

74. A society that fails to invest in its children seeks its own demise.

∽

75. Tolerance is a counterintuitive term to be replaced by inclusivity.

76. People of strong character and principle may perish but never oppressed.

❦

77. Believing in compromise does not mean compromising your beliefs.

❦

78. Forgiveness is a powerful medicine; a grain of it can dissolve a mountain of hatred and betrayal.

79. Some people are quick in criticizing and slow in helping to solve the problem.

80. Plan without passion is like a vehicle without an engine. Passion without a plan is having no vehicle at all.

81. Never underestimate the pain of a broken heart; seek to mitigate it.

82. Life is like a portrait; you can paint it however you choose.

૪

83. Get caught up in the web of power and prestige and watch your life wither away.

૪

84. If this world was not loyal to pharaohs of Egypt, Kings of Persia and Caesars of Rome, will it be to us?

85. When it comes to friends, quality tramples quantity.

♾

86. Like wine true friendship gets better with age.

♾

87. If you want to appreciate the value of time, watch a sunset or a river flow.

88. Everyone wants to have freedom but very few are willing to pay for it.

☙

89. Arrogance and ignorance go hand in hand.

☙

90. Your gut feeling or intuition may not be perfect but it is sometimes the only option you have.

91. Where there is no respect, there is no peace.

✌

92. Protecting the vulnerable is not charity, it is a human responsibility.

✌

93. Alienating and labeling a community for the misdeed of a few is unfair and unwise.

94. I learned to stand up after falling from infants.

⁂

95. A mentor to a pupil is what a gardener is to a flower.

⁂

96. Three indisputable instruments of a meaningful life: humility, hope and hard work.

⁂

97. It is not always who you know but who you avoid.

Nanny's Pearls

98. True freedom is when we are free in spirit, free to choose and free from worldly belongings.

99. No distance is far for connected hearts; nowhere is near when hearts are apart.

100. When you eliminate the superficial elements, you will see the depth of what really matters.

101. Vitality of the Human spirit is predicated on its relentless pursuit of knowledge and wisdom.

※

102. Hesitation is not synonymous with vacillation.

※

103. A leader's character is defined by how he or she brings people to their senses and not play on their emotions.

Nanny's Pearl

My first grade class picture in Karim-Abad: front row, fourth from the right. Our teacher is in official education corps military uniform.

104. So long as there is ignorance and poverty, there will be extremism and violence.

105. If you feel a knot in your throat, a tear in your eye and a stern look on your face when you see a fellow human being in despair, you may be having the signs and symptoms of humanity.

106. There is not such a thing as "small" act of kindness.

Nanny's Pearls

107. A society that tolerates corruption and nepotism dwells in dictatorship.

※

108. We are surrounded by heroes. They are so transparent that we fail to see them.

※

109. There is wisdom and beauty in every kernel of corn, every drop of rain and every grain of sand.

110. Love is a universal language that needs no interpreter nor a dictionary.

⸮

111. Faith and courage are the critical ingredients to any major accomplishment.

⸮

112. Patience, determination, and self-confidence are the indispensable tenets of a successful life.

Nanny's Pearls

113. Spend less time on criticizing and more on praising people's efforts and contributions.

☙

114. Your religion is determined by geography, your faith by you.

☙

115. No challenge, no character.

116. Phrases like: I beg to differ, in my humble opinion or I told you so, display arrogance and are best avoided.

✂

117. Be graceful and magnanimous to someone who genuinely acknowledges his or her mistake.

✂

118. Treat your friends like pedals of a delicate flower.

119. Maintain a healthy distance from some of those who preach so sanctimoniously.

⁂

120. A content spirit envies nobody.

⁂

121. Be generous in sharing your knowledge; for unshared knowledge is a lost treasure.

122.   Not so trusting to be vulnerable and not too prudent to be suspicious.

⁂

123.   Hope is the instrument of the optimist.

⁂

124.   Every land is home, everyone a kin; when the hearts speak thy language in.

Nanny's Pearls

125. Myth: opportunity of a lifetime. Reality: life is full of opportunities.

⁂

126. Those who give the most to the world often have the least to give.

⁂

127. Be quick in learning and patient in teaching.

128. Peace is practiced, not preached.

⚜

129. Kindness to all is humanity, kindness to a few is hypocrisy.

⚜

130. The greatest lessons of life are neither written no spoken; they are lived.

131. Most meaningful communications are non-verbal, the rest is just talk.

132. When your donkey crosses the bridge, be grateful and leave the bridge intact.

133. Don't be impressed so much by the glamour and the hype; remember that, "thunder makes the noise but it is the rain that feeds the grass calmly".

134. If you must, reprimand should be strictly private, tenaciously respectful and very brief.

⁂

135. Patience is a form of wisdom.

⁂

136. Do what you know and don't do what you don't know.

Nanny's Pearls

137. Don't limit your vision only to what your eyes can see.

✃

138. Don't try to gain stature by stepping on others.

✃

139. Human dignity is much like a delicate glass; handle it with care.

✃

140. Taming the demon within is the greatest form of strength.

141. Our past is our best and most expensive teacher; we simply can't afford not to learn from it.

⁂

142. A dream without determination is like a knife without a handle; it does not quite cut it.

⁂

143. Like seasons of the year the stages of our lives have their special colors and characters.

144. Working is not limited to making a living but living to make a difference.

⸜

145. When the rope is around your neck, stop pulling.

⸜

146. All learning begins with imitation; real growth requires innovation.

147. A gate is not a hindrance for the thief but a reminder for the decent.

☙

148. Restraint is an instrument for peace and a character for the wise.

☙

149. Experience is the price paid for a mistake.

Nanny's Pearls

150. Getting in the game takes skill, staying in the game takes character.

⁂

151. Motivation born out of fear is possible but precarious.

⁂

152. Commitment and integrity are the great attributes of a strong leader.

153. Abusing people's trust is the worst form of betrayal.

⁂

154. Unbridled adventurism is not to be confused with courage and valor.

⁂

155. Don't promise a child what you cannot deliver.

⁂

156. Sometimes life feels like a war zone and dodging bullets.

157. With optimism the flickering candle of hope is still aflame despite the adversity.

∞

158. Respect and fairness are the strong pillars of any relationship.

∞

159. If you have to work so hard to fit in a place, chances are that it isn't fit for you; go where you are welcome.

Kamiab Delfanian

With my wife Christina and daughters Shaydah (standing) and Shahrzad on the shore of the Caspian Sea.

160. A hungry stomach has no religion.

✢

161. Be wise with the choices that you make, there is no need to climb every hill.

✢

162. Most of teaching and learning happens outside of classrooms.

163. Human relationship is much like banking accounts: casual acquaintance as checking; common friendship as saving and close friends as trust fund.

⁂

164. No personal gain is worth breaking an innocent heart.

⁂

165. Two types of news travel slowly: scandal of the powerful and death of the poor.

166. Strive to do good, for that is the essence of humanity.

ஃ

167. He who believes in compromise understands the value of peace.

ஃ

168. There is a difference between a teacher and a mentor; ask any student.

169. Distance yourself from profanity.

❧

170. When pursuing a dream keep your eyes on the horizon and let the rays of hope shine upon you.

❧

171. All work is honorable, a hundred pennies make a dollar.

Nanny's Pearls

172. Celebrate your challenges with a toast of creativity.

⁂

173. When you find yourself on a treacherous road, slow down.

⁂

174. Standing up for your own rights takes courage. Standing for the rights of others takes conviction.

175. Life is not a chemistry lab; you don't have to react to every action.

⚜

176. Embrace the imperfect life as there is no perfect one.

⚜

177. When you forget to hear the sound of a river flow and to see a sunset glow, it is life that you have let go.

Nanny's Pearls

178. Remember those who helped you climb up the mountain.

⁂

179. You may get a donkey through a turbulent creek but not a single word through the head of an idiot.

⁂

180. It is good to stand out but you don't want to look like a donkey in a herd of cows.

181. Don't delegate to others tasks that you can do yourself.

❧

182. Knowing what you don't like is just as important as knowing what you do like.

❧

183. Don't take yourself too seriously; for a king and a peasant ultimately share the same destiny.

184. Life does not come with a tool kit.

185. No masterfully-built mansion is worth breaking an innocent heart.

186. As humans we are much like branches of the same tree and waters of the same river, though we may have different roots and flow in different streams.

187. A grain of optimism can change the taste of our lives.

❦

188. Freedom is like the sun; it may be obscured by cloud of oppression but never extinguished.

❦

189. Never underestimate the power of an individual's will.

190. It is far better to live in a hut with dignity than a mansion in disgrace.

❧

191. Patience and persistence are the base of a prosperous life triangle.

❧

192. Bringing a smile to a deserving face is the definition of a successful life.

193. No step is too small and no obstacle is too large for a determined mind.

194. What defines an individual's character is not in how glamorous or painful his win or defeat is but in how he fights the game.

195. Arguing with a fool is like reciting poetry in the ears of a donkey.

196. Patriotism and cultural identity are symbols of pride and distinction. Hatred and bigotry are hallmarks of arrogance and ignorance.

197. Don't mistake fame with greatness; for not every shiny shell has pearl.

198. A man who has no courage in the prairie will have none at the hilltop.

199. A charlatan gains no stature with praise and a decent person loses no character by slander.

❦

200. Every flower has its own scent.

❦

201. Be graceful by not bringing the shortcoming of people's past to light.

202. Not everything is worth a sacrifice.

⁂

203. Even the toughest rock cracks under pressure.

⁂

204. A relationship without trust is like a ship without a compass.

⁂

205. True loyalty is born out of genuine commitment, not a legal responsibility.

206. The value of wealth, wit and wisdom is in how it impacts humanity.

⁂

207. Sometimes you end up trading a horse for a donkey.

⁂

208. Fool me once, shame on you. Fool me twice, still shame on you.

209. Instilling hope in others is a priceless gift.

⸘

210. Trust in god but tie your donkey tight.

⸘

211. Human principle knows no time.

⸘

212. Love is like fire; too close you burn, too far you freeze.

213. Teach your children the virtues of fairness and respect and you have given them the best gift for life.

❦

214. No matter how hard you try, some pots just don't have fitting lids.

❦

215. A bump in the road is a good thing when you "fall asleep".

216. Greed and ignorance have no limits.

⁂

217. The path to genuine love is through respect.

⁂

218. Stop complaining about your surrounding if you lack the will, ability or courage to change it.

219. Do not allow anyone to decide what goals you can or can't achieve.

☙

220. Don't turn a colleague's request for help down unless you have a compelling reason; for it takes a great deal of dignity to ask for help.

☙

221. In business, pressure is cause for pause.

222. A lantern in a peasant's hut may not be a match for a chandelier in a mansion but it still breaks the darkness.

❖

223. A fulfilled life is return on investing in humanity.

❖

224. Don't buy a carpet from anyone until you have a cup of tea with him. (Persian proverb).

Kamiab Delfanian

My sister Nasreen and I in Rochester, Minnesota when I was in training at the Mayo Clinic.